THE JOURNEY TO THE
NORTH POLE

Mike Rosen

Illustrated by Doug Post

The Bookwright Press
New York · 1990

Great Journeys

Frontispiece *The argument between Robert Peary and Frederick Cook as to who first reached the North Pole continued for many years.*

Cover *At his seventh attempt, on April 6, 1909, Robert Peary is generally acknowledged to have been the first explorer to reach the North Pole. He had lived with the Inuit, from whom he learned survival techniques and how to handle a team of huskies.*

First published in the
United States in 1990 by
The Bookwright Press
387 Park Avenue South
New York, NY 10016

First published in 1990 by
Wayland (Publishers) Limited
61 Western Road, Hove
East Sussex BN3 1JD, England

Library of Congress Cataloging-in-Publication Data
Rosen, Mike.
The journey to the North Pole / by Mike Rosen.
    p. cm. — (Great journeys)
Includes bibliographical references.
Summary: Chronicles the hardships faced by explorers trying to reach the North Pole, focusing on Peary and Henson's successful attempt in 1909.
    ISBN 0–531–18344–0
    1. Peary, Robert E. (Robert Edwin), 1856–1920 – Juvenile literature.   2. Explorers – United States – Biography – Juvenile literature.   3. North Pole.   [1. North Pole.   2. Peary, Robert E. (Robert Edwin), 1856–1920.   3. Explorers.]   I. Title   II. Series.
G635.P4R67   1990
919.804′092 – dc20
[B]   89–4

Typeset by DP Press Ltd, Sevenoaks, Kent
Printed in Italy by G. Canale & C.S.p.A., Turin

Contents

Robert Peary

Over a period of twenty-three years Robert Peary explored the frozen lands of the Arctic. Through these years he faced death many times – from starvation, frostbite or fierce blizzards. Despite the dangers, Peary could not stay away from the Arctic. He was determined to succeed in a mission he had dreamed of for years – to reach the North Pole.

Born in the United States in 1856, Peary worked as a surveyor for the U.S. Navy. One of his most important tasks took him to Central America. A large canal was being planned to cross the narrow strip of land there that separates the Atlantic and Pacific oceans. By 1885 Peary was exploring the jungles of Nicaragua to find a possible route for the canal. The work continued until 1887, but in 1886 Peary took a vacation in Greenland. During this trip, he decided to pursue his dream of exploring the Arctic.

By 1886 there had already been many expeditions to explore the Arctic region. The dangers and difficulties were well known. Air temperatures as low as minus 58°F (minus 50°C) are common. In such low temperatures human flesh begins to freeze. Even with warm boots and clothing it is easy for toes and fingers to get

Right *Peary and Cook's routes.*

Above *Robert Peary*

Right *An Inuit hunter and his team of huskies.*

Above *In summer, the Arctic ice melts and breaks up.*

frostbitten. Without medical treatment frostbite can cause gangrene. Until recently the only treatment for gangrene was to amputate the affected parts of the body.

The Arctic weather presents many other dangers. The fierce winds and cold dry air suck all the moisture from the skin. Blizzards can last for several days, forcing travelers to shelter in snow caves. When the storm is over, the land can look completely different, and vital food and fuel dumps may be buried in fresh snow. The snow may also hide deep and dangerous crevasses.

To make Arctic exploration even more difficult, there is only a short time each year when it is possible to travel in the far north of the Arctic. For several months in winter there is little daylight, and it is difficult to

work outside for long periods. Between May and late August the sun's heat melts the icecap that covers the Polar Sea, turning it into a dangerous mixture of icebergs, floes and channels of deep water hidden under slush or thin ice.

Arctic explorers have another problem. It is difficult to know exactly when they have found the North Pole. The position of the North Pole is 90 degrees north of the Equator. This is not the same point as Magnetic North, to which a compass points. At 90 degrees north, in the middle of the Arctic Ocean, there is no fixed land. The pack ice drifts on the ocean currents, sometimes traveling many miles each day. Instead of using a compass to check their position, the early explorers worked with a sextant, using the position of the sun or stars.

Peoples of the Arctic

Left *A team of huskies on the pack ice. Before he could explore the Arctic safely, Peary had to learn dog-handling skills. The Inuit taught him how to control a team of dogs pulling a sledge across rough ice.*

The Far North is too barren an area for humans to live in for long periods. Farther south, on the coasts of Greenland and the countries around the Arctic Ocean, people have lived comfortably for thousands of years. These are the Inuit. They have developed a way of living that is perfectly suited to the Arctic climate. Robert Peary was one of the first explorers to realize this and use the Inuit's knowledge and methods of travel to help him on his journeys. Peary was lucky that the Inuit were happy to share their knowledge with him. Without their help his explorations, like so many earlier expeditions, might have ended in disaster.

In the 1880s, when Peary began his Arctic travels, the Inuit lived by hunting and fishing. From eider ducks, caribou, seals, whales and bears they gained everything they needed to live: food, fuel from blubber and fats, and clothing from the skins. During the winter the Inuit lived in villages. Their huts were made

Above *Igloos were used mainly on hunting expeditions, which took the Inuit far away from their winter houses. Igloos are made from blocks of snow, which fit together so tightly that even a small oil lamp can keep the inside warm.*

of stone and turf. Some groups built igloos with blocks of solid ice. Through the spring and summer they could catch plenty of fish. In summer many Inuit followed the animals they were hunting and moved from place to place, living in tents.

The Inuit Peary met used survival skills that had been developed over thousands of years. They understood the weather patterns that warned of blizzards, and the seasonal changes that affected the animals, fish and birds they hunted. With their sledges hauled by teams of dogs, the Inuit traveled long distances across the frozen seas in winter, using the position of the stars to guide them. In summer the coastal Inuit would use kayaks and bigger boats to hunt at sea.

They knew how to find the easiest routes across the pack ice in winter and the way through the icebergs and drifting floes in summer.

Today there are many Inuit still living on the edges of the Arctic. Few of them live in the traditional way Peary saw. Most Inuit work on the big factory fishing ships, at the oil-drilling sites in Alaska, or in the towns and ports that support these industries. Military bases have been built in many parts of the Arctic by the United States and the USSR. Those Inuit who still live by hunting and fishing use motor boats and snowmobiles to travel, and they hunt with expensive equipment. While some Inuit prefer the new way of life, others are dismayed by the loss of traditional skills.

Below *The Inuit respect wildlife. They depend on Arctic animals to help them to survive. Traditionally, every part of any animal they kill is used for food, clothing or tools. The feathers of the eider duck (shown below) are used to fill the linings of jackets to give them extra warmth.*

Early European Explorers

Left *In 1776, Captain James Cook, the British explorer of the Pacific Ocean, tried to follow the coast of Alaska eastward from the Bering Straits.*

The first Europeans to visit the Arctic were the Vikings, who settled on the coasts of Greenland in the tenth century. At that time the Arctic climate was much warmer than it is today, and the Vikings lived by raising cattle. Occasionally they had contact with the Inuit who lived farther north. After several hundred years, in the fourteenth century, a new Ice Age began. Unlike the Inuit, the Vikings were unable to develop the skills needed to make life in the Arctic possible. Eventually the Viking settlements had died out.

The next explorers were the British, French and Dutch, searching for a way to Asia. Europeans valued the rich silks and spices that came from China, but after the collapse of the Mongol Empire in 1368, the overland Silk Route for trade was blocked by wars between rival rulers. Spanish and Portuguese traders controlled the sea routes to China around South America and Africa. The British, French and Dutch hoped they could find a new route across the Arctic Ocean that would take them directly to China.

At first, these early explorers went north around the coast of Norway and along the northern shores of Asia. This route was known as the Northeast Passage. By the end of the sixteenth century this Northeast Passage became blocked as the pack ice spread farther south. Explorers then began to search for the Northwest Passage, which they hoped ran from Greenland across the northern coast of Canada to the Bering Straits.

During the next two centuries men such as William Baffin, Henry Hudson and Alexander Mackenzie mapped the seas and coasts off the northeast tip of Canada. Captain James Cook, the British sailor who had spent many years exploring the Pacific Ocean, sailed up the coast of Alaska and through the Bering Straits in an attempt to find the Northwest Passage

from the western end (1776–9). None of these explorers found the Northwest Passage. Cook was forced to turn back before his ships were crushed by the thick winter ice. Hudson's last voyage ended tragically when his crew mutinied, leaving Hudson, his young son and several loyal crew members cast adrift in a small boat.

Although they did not find the Northwest Passage, these explorers learned much that was useful. Their maps helped later expeditions find the best routes. Through living in the Arctic, the early explorers learned how to deal with some of the problems caused by the extreme cold and the barren landscape. Merchants followed the explorers and started a trade with the Inuit in furs, sealskins and whale products. Whaling ships used the new maps to venture farther north.

Left *As explorers mapped the maze of islands and channels off Greenland, whaling ships followed them farther north in the hunt for whales. This illustration shows such a ship in action in 1851.*

Arctic Disaster

The nineteenth century started well for Arctic explorers. In 1818 John Ross discovered the beginning of a possible Northwest Passage. Nine years later William Parry tried to reach the North Pole. Starting from the island of Spitsbergen, Parry struggled across the icecap but finally realized that the pack ice was drifting south on the ocean current faster than he was moving north. Although he did not reach the Pole, Parry had gone farther north than any other explorer. In 1831 James Ross discovered the location of Magnetic North off the coast of Canada.

Then in 1845 Sir John Franklin sailed from London with 130 men in two ships in another attempt to find the Northwest Passage. Franklin was an experienced Arctic explorer. He had already sailed through many of the channels that made up the entrance to the Northwest Passage. On another expedition he had gone overland from Hudson Bay to map a long stretch of the Arctic coast of Canada. Franklin believed that less than 60 miles (97 km) of the Northwest Passage remained to be found: that which lay along the coast of King William Land.

Franklin's expedition was well prepared. The ships' hulls were strengthened with sheets of iron. Each ship contained a large boiler to heat water, which would be fed through a system of pipes to warm the living space during the Arctic winter. Food supplies for three years were carried as well as medical equipment.

Below *After their ships had been crushed in the pack ice, Franklin's sailors tried to walk to safety across the frozen ocean. Weak from disease and hunger, they died a horrible death.*

In September 1845, Franklin settled down for the winter on Devon Island. Although three sailors died between January and April, there seemed no cause for alarm. The ships' doctors agreed the men had died from common diseases. When the pack ice thawed, Franklin's ships sailed down the west coast of King William Land. Unfortunately this was a dangerous mistake. Soon they were trapped in thick ice, which failed to melt that summer.

Things quickly moved from bad to worse. Over the winter of 1846–7 twenty-six sailors died and in June, 1847, Franklin died also. The doctors could not explain the cause of these deaths. Rumors and fear spread fast among the crews trapped on their ships in the frozen ocean. When the ice failed to melt again in the summer of 1848, the expedition abandoned the ships. The new plan was to cross King William Land and follow the Back River to a trading post at the Great Salt Lake.

None of Franklin's sailors escaped the Arctic. Weak from disease and starvation, they died before they reached the Back River. Search parties sent from Britain in the 1850s found the evidence of the terrible end of Franklin's expedition. The last starving men had turned to cannibalism, eating the bodies of those who had died.

From Disaster to Success

Strangely, the terrible fate of Franklin's expedition began a period of success for Arctic explorers. The search parties from Britain and the United States completed the maps of Canada's Arctic coast. In 1853 Captain McClure's sailors made the first journey through the Northwest Passage, by walking east after abandoning their ship at the western edge of the pack ice. The searchers made another sad discovery. They found that King William Land was in fact an island and the pack ice was quite thin on its eastern coast. If Franklin had sailed down the east coast of the island, his ships would not have been trapped. The Norwegian explorer Roald Amundsen finally sailed the whole Northwest Passage by this route in 1908.

Even if he had found the right route, it is unlikely that Franklin could have succeeded. Scientists from Canada have examined the bodies of the three sailors who died during the expedition's first winter. Perfectly preserved in the cold Arctic ground, these bodies showed clear evidence that one of the causes of death was lead poisoning. The lead came from the soldered seams of the cans containing the expedition's food. Everything the sailors ate from cans was slowly killing them.

After 1860 explorers turned their interest from the Northwest Passage to the North Pole. An American, Charles Hall, and the British sailor Sir George Nares sailed as far north as possible along the coasts of Greenland. Thick pack ice blocked their routes, and it seemed as if the only way to the

Above *Charles Hall was one of the first Americans to attempt long explorations by sledge.*

Left *Sir John Franklin died in 1847. In searching for his expedition, rescuers finally found the Northwest Passage.*

Far left *140 years after his death, the body of John Hartnell, one of Franklin's crew, was found, almost perfectly preserved in the frozen Arctic soil. Canadian scientists who examined the body found clear signs of lead poisoning.*

Inset *Sir George Nares*

Below *Fridtjof Nansen*

Above *Peary's team of huskies were to be vital to the success of his expedition to the pole.*

North Pole was overland. Hall made several journeys through Greenland by sledge. Although he learned many useful things about the problems of sledge travel, Hall got no farther than 82 degrees north before his death in 1871.

In 1888 the Norwegian explorer Fridtjof Nansen achieved a great success. With two friends he crossed Greenland from coast to coast by sledge. The journey took nearly four months of hard struggle. Nansen found that the center of Greenland was a wild and barren plateau situated over 800 feet (2,400 m) above sea level. Even though he was traveling in summer, Nansen suffered terribly from the extreme cold. Without dogs to haul their sledges, Nansen and his friends found it difficult to cover even a short distance each day, especially on the climb up to the high plateau and where the ice was rough. Only the final part of their journey was easier, riding the sledges downhill using sails to catch the wind. Nansen's journey convinced Peary that he could journey overland to the Pole, if the icecap stretched far enough.

First Impressions: 1886-92

After his trip to Greenland in 1886, Peary was unable to return to the Arctic until 1891. He knew that he could not hope to reach the Pole on his first journey. He needed experience in Arctic travel, and part of his plan for 1891 was to learn survival skills from the Inuit. Peary was convinced that the Pole could only be reached by a small party carrying as little baggage as possible and living as the Inuit did.

With Peary in 1891 were five other men and his wife, Josephine. Before the expedition left, many people said that life in the Arctic would be too hard for a woman. Josephine Peary was scornful of their views, reminding them that the Arctic was home to thousands of Inuit women who lived there all year round. Another member of the party was Matthew Henson. Henson had been employed as Peary's personal assistant since 1885. Peary grew to rely on Henson's strength, determination and skill. Henson was the first black person to play a vital role in Arctic exploration.

Below *Walrus hunting was a dangerous way to find food. A large walrus could easily damage small boats and kayaks.*

The expedition doctor, Frederick Cook, soon had work to do. On the voyage north Peary's right leg was broken in an accident. For six weeks after they arrived in Greenland, Peary was unable to walk. He used the time to make contact with a local Inuit village. The Inuit taught Peary and his friends how to make clothes from animal skins, which would keep them alive in a blizzard. When his leg healed, Peary learned to drive a sledge pulled by a dog team.

Before winter arrived Peary and his friends built themselves a house from wood and stone. They also went hunting to get enough meat to feed them through the winter. On one expedition they were attacked by a herd of a hundred walrus, whose fierce tusks could easily damage the small boats. A desperate battle began, but the explorers' rifles killed many walrus and the rest quickly fled.

In the spring of 1892 Peary made many short trips to practice the skills he had learned. On one of these he was nearly killed when the roof of his igloo collapsed during a storm. Then, in May, full of excitement, Peary and a traveling companion began their first long journey. They battled through blizzards and gales, sometimes having to shelter in their igloos for several days. The dogs caused endless trouble, fighting among themselves and biting anyone who tried to harness them to the sledges. Despite the problems, Peary managed to cover a distance of 500 miles (800 km), reaching a place he named Independence Bay. There was no time for further traveling before Peary's return to the United States, but he was already planning his next Arctic expedition.

Beaten by Storms: 1893-4

Peary's expedition of 1893 was much larger than his first one. The plan was for support parties to lay supply dumps along the first part of the route north and cut a path through any serious obstacles on the way. A small group led by Peary would follow this route to its end and then explore as far north as possible.

Immediately the plan went wrong. Wild storms kept the support parties from laying out the route, and three sledges left on the ice were simply blown away and lost. Even worse was to come. During one storm a gigantic iceberg was blown over outside Bowdoin Bay where the expedition was based. It created an enormous tidal wave that raced into the bay, heading straight for the beach. The force of the wave hurled the expedition's whaleboat 330 feet (100 m) through the air, smashing it to matchwood on the icy cliffs. Down on the shore the wave swept over the vital stocks of fuel oil. Peary watched in horror and despair as the undertow dragged the precious barrels of oil out into the waters of the bay.

Below *A gigantic tidal wave swept across the beach, smashing sledges and boats and destroying the expedition's fuel supplies.*

The winter seemed even colder than usual, and the small store of fuel oil had to be used carefully. Josephine Peary had given birth to a baby girl in September but the child seemed not to suffer from the cold. Luckily there was plenty of fresh meat and fish, and everyone stayed cheerful.

As soon as the days grew light again, Peary went out with the support parties to help place the supply dumps. Once more, violent storms held them back. The route lay along a glacier. Its surface was rough and covered with a layer of soft snow that hid a number of deadly crevasses. With the snow whirling around them in the gusting gale, Peary and his men struggled with the sledges. They pushed them through snowdrifts and lifted them over large hummocks. The dog teams became exhausted, and on one day the group could travel only 4 km (2 and one-half miles).

As the storms grew worse, Peary and his men were forced to shelter in their tents. For three days they waited. On the fourth day the wind dropped, and Peary led them on. They made almost 4 miles (6 km) that day before the storm returned. One of the tents began to leak and two of the men got frostbite. All eight huddled together in the last tent while the wind howled and the temperature fell to minus 45°F (minus 43°C). Despite the storms, Peary forced the group onward, but the end was near. When another storm trapped them in their tents for three days, Peary had had enough. Defeated by the Arctic weather, they turned back.

Above *Despite their efforts, Peary and his men were forced to retreat by violent storms. The weather conditions were terrifying and the men quickly became exhausted.*

Starvation: 1895

Only Peary, Henson and Hugh Lee stayed at Bowdoin Bay for the winter of 1894. In March 1895 these three set out once again by sledge for the Far North, with six Inuit guides. Their supplies of food were small, but they hoped to find the store dumps left on the glacier the year before. Unfortunately the first food dump was buried beneath thick ice. The same problem faced them at the second dump. Peary sent the Inuit guides back to their homes and talked with Lee and Henson. He told them that they had enough food to reach Independence Bay. There they could find musk oxen: to hunt for fresh meat. Bravely they decided to carry on despite the shortage of food supplies.

Soon they were stopped by another storm. For two days they shivered in their tent. Then

Lee became ill and could march only a short distance each day. With these delays, their food began to run short far from Independence Bay. Lee stayed behind while the other two men desperately struggled on. At last the ground began to slope downhill. Ahead they could see the strip of land along the coast that was Independence Bay. Through the thick snowdrifts they stumbled, often sinking in the deep snow. They trudged down across the tumbled rocks, bruising their bodies on the rough boulders. At last they reached the plain, eager to find food. To their horror, the musk oxen were gone.

Peary knew they were in serious danger. Frantically he searched for any sign of the animals while Henson built a camp. When the exhausted Lee finally arrived at the tents, all three men collapsed and slept for nearly two days.

When they awoke, Lee was too weak to move. Peary and Henson took the remaining dogs and food and left in search of musk oxen. After some anxious hours the starving men found fresh animal tracks in the snow. These led to a large herd of musk oxen, many of which were soon shot. Around midnight Peary and Henson returned to Lee at the camp and all three feasted on the raw meat.

During Peary's two years of struggle, the Norwegian explorer Fridtjof Nansen had been busy. He had had a ship built with rounded sides that the pack ice could not grip and crush. On this ship, the *Fram*, Nansen floated in the pack ice for eighteen months. When he saw that he would not drift over the Pole, Nansen tried to cover the last stage by sledge and kayak. He got within 233 miles (360 km) of the Pole before turning back toward Norway.

A New Approach: 1898

Left *Major Adolphus Washington Greely led one of America's most disastrous Arctic expeditions. In 1884, seventeen of Greely's men died in their winter camp at Fort Conger.*

Far left *Lord Northcliffe, the British newspaper owner, lent Peary a yacht,* Windward, *for his expedition of 1898.*

Nansen's near-success and Peary's own failures forced him to think hard about his methods of travel. He decided that it would be best to sail farther north before starting the sledge journey. Lord Northcliffe, owner of the *Daily Mail* newspaper, gave Peary his yacht *Windward* that had just returned from an Arctic voyage with Nansen.

In the *Windward*, Peary sailed as far as Kane Basin on the shores of Ellesmere Land. By November 1898 Peary had built huts for the winter, prepared stocks of food and fuel, and placed a supply dump 80 miles (130 km) north of his base. On December 20, 1898, in the darkness of the Arctic midwinter, Peary set out on a trek 250 miles (400 km) north to Fort Conger. At Fort Conger was a hut that had been built by the American explorer Major Adolphus Washington Greely in the 1850s. Peary hoped it would be in good enough condition to use as his base for an attempt to reach the North Pole.

The journey was nearly another disaster. As before, Peary and his men found themselves trapped in their tents by violent storms. On the few days when the raging winds were quiet, deep snow made it hard to keep the sledges moving. The surface of the ice was a frozen tangle of hummocks, ridges, crevasses and ice cliffs. It was hard enough by moonlight, but when the moon no longer shone it became nearly impossible to avoid accidents. Despite severe frostbite in his feet, Peary kept going. Just as it seemed that they would run out of food they reached Fort Conger. Luckily the hut was in good condition, with stores of food inside.

Peary was not so lucky with his frostbite. He became unable to walk, and exploration north of Fort Conger was stopped. Instead, strapped to a sledge, Peary made the hard journey back to his base on Ellesmere Land. There the expedition doctor cut off eight of Peary's toes to prevent gangrene. The doctor thought Peary would never walk properly again. Peary thought otherwise, and despite the intense pain, he was back at Fort Conger after only six weeks' rest.

Between 1899 and 1902 Peary used Fort Conger as his base. He made one journey directly out toward the North Pole but had to turn back when warm weather melted the pack ice. Peary also explored the northern coast of Greenland; he proved both that it was an island and that it was no good as a starting point for a journey to the North Pole. He came to realize that he should start from the northern coast of Grinnell Land, north of Ellesmere Land. In order for this plan to succeed, he needed an even better ship than the *Windward*.

Below *When Peary used Greely's camp at Fort Conger in 1898, he too met with disaster. Suffering from severe frostbite, Peary was lucky to survive the return journey, strapped to a sledge.*

Peary Tries Again: 1905

It took Peary three years to organize another expedition to the Arctic. A new ship was built with a strengthened hull and more powerful engines. The rudder could be retracted into the hull to protect it if ice trapped the ship. Finally there was a winch, driven by the main engines, which would be able to pull the ship through sections of thin pack ice.

The new ship, named *Roosevelt*, proved its worth in 1905. Its captain, Bob Bartlett, was able to steer it through the difficult channels off the coast of Greenland and land Peary on the northeastern shores of Ellesmere Land. This was almost as far north as Peary had ever been before. As Peary's team spent the winter at Cape Sheridan, they felt sure this time they would reach the Pole.

Peary no longer believed that small groups had the best chance of success. His experience of the Arctic had shown that the great distances to be traveled over the barren icecap in such a harsh climate rapidly weakened even the strongest explorers. There was no possibility of living by hunting and fishing in the Far North. This was proved by the fact that no Inuit lived there.

For 1905–6 Peary planned to use a system of support groups. Each group would go forward a set distance with a load of supplies, leaving at intervals of a day. Using some of the supplies left by the earlier group, each party would get a

Below *In 1905 Peary tried a new system. He used support parties to set up supply dumps along the route so that he and Henson could race for the pole without having to carry heavy loads.*

little farther. Eventually, a network of supply dumps would stretch across the pack ice toward the North Pole. Then the final group could travel without heavy loads, living off the supply dumps and saving their strength for the last stage of the journey.

In the spring of 1906 the support groups left at intervals as planned. Within a few days they were all together again – stopped by a big "lead" of open water as the pack ice broke up in the warmer weather. There was worse news still. The following groups had been unable to find some of the supply dumps placed by the leading parties. Because the ice floes were drifting with the ocean currents, the supply dumps were no longer where they had been left.

Despite the many problems, Peary and Henson decided to try to reach the Pole without the support groups. One night, as thin ice covered the lead, they crossed over to the far side. For several days they made good progress. Then they realized that if they went farther their food would run out before they could get back to base. Wisely they turned back. Even so, the drifting floes took them off their route and they were lucky to reach land before their supplies failed. Once again the Arctic had defeated Peary.

Planning for Success: 1908

Left *Peary's ship, the* Roosevelt, *was specially designed to survive the dangers of sailing through pack ice. It had a strengthened hull and a retractable rudder.*

Below *Peary on board the* Roosevelt, *wearing the clothes he wore for exploration. These had been made by the Inuit.*

Peary thought carefully about the problems that had beaten him in 1906. During 1907 he organized an even bigger expedition while waiting for the *Roosevelt* to be refitted and overhauled. Part of Peary's plan was to spend the first winter moving supplies from Cape Sheridan to Cape Columbia. This was the closest land to the North Pole and too far into the pack ice for the *Roosevelt* to reach. Peary hoped that by working through the winter he would be able to set off for the Pole earlier in the year. This would give him more time before the warm weather broke up the pack ice into dangerous floes and leads.

To deal with the problem of the drifting floes, Peary planned a new system for the support parties. All the groups would

travel together but turn back one by one as the supplies they carried were used. Those groups detailed to turn back first would be given the biggest loads on the outward journey. One party had the job of traveling ahead each day to build a camp for the others to use. A base would be built halfway to the Pole. Another support team would stay there to meet any group returning from an attempt to reach the Pole. If the base seemed to be drifting on the currents, the support team there would move it back to its original place.

While Peary was planning his expedition he heard worrying news. Dr. Frederick Cook had left on a voyage of exploration to the Arctic. Cook had been the doctor on Peary's first expedition to Greenland in 1891. Since then he had traveled in Antarctica, Alaska and Arctic Canada. Peary was afraid that Cook would reach the North Pole before him. After all

his years of hard work, Peary was determined to be first to the North Pole.

Cook began his voyage in 1907. Peary had to wait anxiously through the winter and spring of 1908 before the *Roosevelt* was ready. As soon as possible Peary sailed north. By September 1908 the *Roosevelt* had reached the planned winter base at Cape Sheridan. On the way Peary had found Cook's base in Greenland. Some Inuit there told him that Cook was definitely trying to reach the North Pole but had only two Inuit to help him. Peary felt sure that Cook could never reach the Pole from Greenland with such a small expedition. As his plan to move supplies to Cape Columbia went smoothly, Peary relaxed. He felt sure he would not fail this time and that he would soon be the first person to reach the North Pole.

A Difficult Start: 1909

Early on February 28, 1909, the first support groups left Cape Columbia. In the frosty air the breath from the dog teams created a white mist of steam around the sledges. As the fur-clad explorers skimmed across the frozen ground on their skis, Peary watched with satisfaction. A few hours later a second group followed them. Peary left the next day, after finally checking that all was going according to plan.

The start of the journey was hard. Where the pack ice neared land, it was squeezed into a smaller space. This pressure caused the ice to bulge into hummocks and ridges, some of which were nearly 100 feet (30 m) high. The first groups had found or cut a way through these, but the surface of the passageways remained very uneven. As they raced across the corrugated surface, Peary's sledges suffered constant damage. Several times there were accidents as the sledges overturned. In one of these the fuel cans were damaged, and Peary watched in horror as precious fuel leaked over the ice.

Below *As the ice gave way, Ross Marvin sank to his death.*

It was now vital to contact the first support group, which would have to return to Cape Columbia and fetch more fuel. That night Peary was halted by a lead of open water. Around midnight the ice on the lead became thick enough for the sledges to cross. On the other side Peary searched anxiously for the trail left by the support groups who were ahead of him. When two trails were found, one of which led back toward Cape Columbia, it was clear that they had missed the first returning support group somewhere along the route. Immediately Peary sent Ross Marvin in pursuit. By great efforts, Ross Marvin reached Cape Columbia in time. Soon the extra fuel was on its way to Peary.

Far ahead Peary did not know whether Ross Marvin had succeeded in his mission. He was afraid of getting too far behind the leading group led by Captain Bartlett but dared not go on without the extra fuel that Ross Marvin was bringing. At the next big lead Peary waited for Ross Marvin to catch up.

After Ross Marvin arrived, Peary's group moved on in pursuit of Bartlett who was several days ahead. The weather became colder again and there were fewer leads to block the way. One by one the support groups turned back toward Cape Columbia. At this point the expedition had its worst accident. On his way back Ross Marvin had to cross a big lead. It was covered with very thin ice. Despite moving very carefully, he fell through the ice and was drowned. Peary went on, not knowing of Ross Marvin's death. Within a few days he had joined Captain Bartlett. The final stage of the journey was about to begin.

Peary at the Pole: 1909

On March 28, 1909, the three groups, led by Peary, Henson and Bartlett, were camping on an ice floe. Suddenly there was a terrifying noise and the floe split in two. Peary and Henson were safe on the main part, but Bartlett was trapped on the smaller section drifting away. As the gap between the floes widened, it looked as though Bartlett's team might be permanently separated from the main group. Luckily the current brought the two floes back together and Bartlett's men scrambled across to safety.

After this narrow escape there were no more problems. Bartlett turned back for Cape Columbia when they reached 88 degrees north. Peary, Henson and four Inuit carried on across rough ground but in good weather. On April 6, 1909, they were 2 miles (3 km) from the North Pole. From this point they moved forward quickly. Henson recorded the details of Peary's observations with the sextant.

Below *Bartlett was stranded alone on the wrong part of an ice floe as the ice split in two. Luckily the two parts floated back together and he was able to scramble across to safety.*

They could never get a precise reading to prove they stood at 90 degrees north because their instruments and calculation tables were not accurate enough. All they felt sure of was that the North Pole lay within the small area of ice they had reached. A snow cairn was built at that spot and the United States flag was placed on top. It was the moment Peary had anticipated for over twenty-three years.

The good weather held, and Peary and Henson were back at Cape Columbia by April 23, 1909. Instead of rushing to tell the world of his success, Peary first took his men on a hunting expedition. This provided winter meat for the Inuit who had helped him. It was September 1909 before Peary reached the coast of Labrador. There he stopped at a fishing port to send news of his achievement to the world. To his fury he heard that five days earlier Dr. Cook had claimed to have reached the North Pole in April 1908 – nearly a year before Peary.

On his return to New York, Peary called Cook a liar and said that Cook had never been to the North Pole. Experts on Arctic exploration in London and Copenhagen supported Cook, but the American public believed Peary. The argument between the two men raged on for many years.

This debate still continues, but many people believe Peary reached the pole. Even today when there are motorized vehicles specially built for Arctic use, and military bases that are situated all over the Arctic to help explorers, very few people have managed to reach this most northerly point, which had so fascinated Peary.

Glossary

Crevasse A split in the surface of a glacier or pack ice. These are often hundreds of feet deep.

Floes Large or small flat sections of floating ice that have broken away from the main pack ice.

Frostbite Freezing of parts of the body, such as fingers and toes. Frostbite keeps blood from flowing through the damaged area and may lead to gangrene.

Gangrene Decay of some part of the body caused when the flow of blood is blocked by injury or disease. Gangrene can spread throughout the body. In Peary's time amputation of the affected limb was the normal treatment.

Hull The framework of a ship.

Hummock A large bump on rough ground.

Icebergs Enormous blocks of ice that have broken away from the pack ice. Most of the ice in an iceberg is underwater.

Lead A channel of open water between sections of pack ice.

Magnetic North The direction toward which the needle of a compass points. Its position has moved since it was first discovered by James Ross in 1831 on King William Land.

Mongol Empire In the thirteenth century most of Asia was ruled by the Mongols, a nomadic people from Central Asia. The empire gradually collapsed from about 1360 as the Chinese and Muslim people of Asia successfully rebelled.

Mutiny The refusal to carry out orders. Today this word is used only to describe rebellion by members of the armed forces. In earlier times it also applied to almost all sailors who refused to follow their captain's decisions.

Pack ice The thick ice that covers the central section of the Polar Seas. In winter it stretches farther south than it does in summer.

Rudder A large flat board or piece of metal fitted underwater at the rear of a ship and turned by the steering gear. The force of water on the rudder is least when rudder and ship are pointing in the same direction. Turning the rudder increases the force of water and makes the ship turn to get back in line with the rudder.

Sextant An instrument for measuring the angle between the observer's position on the earth's surface and the position of the sun above the horizon.

Silk Route The ancient trading route linking Europe and China across Asia. Silk was one of the most important products traded along this route.

Supply dumps Stores of food, fuel and equipment left in a known place for later use.

Support parties People sent out to prepare a route or lay supply dumps to support the main group of explorers. These are sometimes used to help returning explorers over the last stages of the journey back to base.

Surveyor A person whose job it is to measure distances between places and their direction from each other when a map of an area is being made.

Undertow The strong current created by the weight of moving water when a wave returns to sea after reaching the beach.

Winch A cylinder around which rope can be wound to lift or pull a heavy object. The cylinder works like a gear to make lifting or pulling easier. Today most winches are driven by motors.

Finding out More

The Embassies of those countries that border on the Arctic such as Canada, Norway and the USSR are often happy to give you more information about that part of their country. For information about Greenland contact the Embassy of Denmark. If you visit Oslo, the capital of Norway, go and look at the Fram Museum, which is a museum of Polar exploration. The following books may interest you. Ask for them at your local library.

About the Arctic:
Jill Hughes, *A Closer Look at the Arctic Lands*, (Gloucester, 1987)
Jill Hughes, *Eskimos*, (Gloucester, 1984).

P. Jacobsen & P. Kristensen, *A Family in Greenland*, (Bookwright, 1986)
P. Jacobsen & P. Kristensen, *A Family in Iceland*, (Bookwright, 1986)
Cass Sandak, *The Arctic and Antarctic*, (Franklin Watts, 1987)

About the Vikings:
Jill Hughes, *Vikings*, (Gloucester, 1984)
Hazel Martell, *The Vikings*, (Warwick, 1986)
Robin May, *Canute and the Vikings*, (Bookwright, 1985)

About Polar Exploration:
R. Matthews, *Race to the South Pole*, (Bookwright, 1989)

Picture Acknowledgments

The publishers would like to thank the following for allowing their illustrations to be used in this book:
Brian and Cherry Alexander 5 (top right), 6 (top and bottom), 13 (top); Mary Evans Picture Library *frontispiece*, 8 (left), 13 (center and bottom), 20 (left and right); Frank Lane Picture Agency 7; The Mansell Collection 24 (top and bottom), 25 (left and right); Natural Science Photo 5 (bottom); Peter Newark's Western Americana 5 (top left); Ann Ronan Picture Library 9 (bottom), 12 (top and bottom center); Topham Picture Library 8 (right), 12 (bottom left), 29. The map on page 4 is by Peter Bull.

Index